RUSSIA
the land

Greg Nickles

A Bobbie Kalman Book

The Lands, Peoples, and Cultures Series

Crabtree Publishing Company

The Lands, Peoples, and Cultures Series

Created by Bobbie Kalman

Coordinating editor
Ellen Rodger

Project development, editing, and design
First Folio Resource Group, Inc.
  Pauline Beggs
  Tom Dart
  Bruce Krever
  Kathryn Lane
  Debbie Smith

Separations and film
Dot 'n Line Image Inc.

Printer
Worzalla Publishing Company

Consultants
Theodore H. Friedgut; Larissa Kisseleva-van Amsterdam; Bella Kotik-Friedgut; Evgueni Petrusevich, Consulate General, Russian Federation, Montreal; Sergei Ulianitsky; and Paul van Amsterdam

Photographs
B. & C. Alexander/Photo Researchers: p. 28 (top); APA/Archive Photos: p. 30; API/Explorer, The National Audubon Society Collection/Photo Researchers: p. 11 (middle); Peter Arkell/Impact: p. 21 (bottom); CNP/Archive Photos: p. 31 (top); Corbis: p. 31 (bottom); Corbis/Hulton-Deutsch Collection: p. 6 (bottom); Corbis/Wolfgang Kaehler: p. 23 (top left), p. 29 (top); Corbis/Yevgeny Khaldei: p. 7 (top); Corbis/Bob Krist: p. 19 (bottom); Corbis/Steve Raymer: p. 12 (top); Corbis/Galen Rowell: p. 17 (top); Corbis/Gregor Schmid: p. 23 (top right); Corbis/Michael T. Sedam: p. 3; Corbis/Peter Turnley: p. 7 (bottom); Corbis/Ralph White: p. 17 (bottom); Georg Gerster, The National Audubon Society Collection/Photo Researchers: p. 10 (top); Philip Gordon/Impact: p. 25 (bottom); Jeff Greenberg/Photo Researchers: p. 26 (bottom); Mark Henley/Impact: p. 4; Andy Johnstone/Impact: title page, p. 12 (bottom), p. 20 (bottom); Wolfgang Kaehler: cover, p. 5, p. 6 (top), p. 8, p. 10 (bottom), p. 11 (top), p. 13 (top), p. 21 (top right), p. 22 (both), p. 23 (bottom), p. 24 (both), p. 25 (top), p. 27 (top); David Kampfner/Impact: p. 29 (bottom); John Kaprielian, The National Audubon Society Collection/Photo Researchers: p. 15 (top); Paolo Koch/Photo Researchers: p. 16 (top); Tom & Pat Leeson, The National Audubon Society Collection/Photo Researchers: p. 15 (bottom); Material World/Impact: p. 19 (top); Tom McHugh, The National Audubon Society Collection/Photo Researchers: p. 14 (top), p. 16 (bottom); C. Monteath/Hedgehog House/Explorer/Photo Researchers: p. 13 (bottom); Caroline Penn/Impact: p. 20 (top), p. 21 (top left); Jonathan Pile/Impact: p. 18 (bottom); Reuters/Peter Andrews/Archive Photos: p. 27 (bottom); C. Sappa/Hoa-Qui/Photo Researchers: p. 18 (top); Bruce Stephens/Impact: p. 28 (bottom); Roger Tidman, The National Audubon Society Collection/Photo Researchers: p. 11 (bottom), p. 14 (bottom); Janet Wishnetsky/Impact: p. 26 (top); Sarah Worker/Impact: p. 9

Map
Jim Chernishenko

Illustrations
David Wysotski, Allure Illustrations: back cover

Cover: Koryak Volcano looms beyond a marsh on Kamchatka Peninsula.

Title page: The Kremlin sits next to the half-frozen waters of Moskva River.

Icon: *Troikas*, sleighs pulled by three horses, appear at the head of each section.

Back cover: The Kamchatka brown bear is a symbol of Russia.

Published by
Crabtree Publishing Company

PMB 16A
350 Fifth Avenue
Suite 3308
New York
N.Y. 10118

612 Welland Avenue
St. Catharines,
Ontario, Canada
L2M 5V6

73 Lime Walk
Headington
Oxford OX3 7AD
United Kingdom

Cataloging in Publication Data
Nickles, Greg, 1969-
  Russia--the land/ Greg Nickles.
    p.cm.--(Lands, peoples and cultures series)
  Includes index.
  Summary: Introduces the land of Russia, including the country's geography, history, industry, agriculture, and wildlife.
    ISBN 0-86505-239-7 (RLB) -- ISBN 086505-318-9 (pbk.)
    1. Russia (Federation)--Juvenile literature. [1. Russia (Federation)] I. Title. II. Series.

DK510.23.N53 2000
947--dc21   LC 00-056154

Contents

 Old and new

The Russian Federation, more commonly known as Russia, is the world's largest country. This vast, wintry land is filled with the old and new. Russia's history goes back over a thousand years. The country, however, has existed in its present form only since 1991.

Today, Russians are making great changes to their nation. In the wilderness, they are constructing new communities and mining **natural resources**. In the cities, new businesses and flashy advertising signs from the West now stand beside old churches with onion-shaped domes. These opposites make Russia truly unique.

Facts at a glance

Official name: Russian Federation
Capital city: Moscow
Population: 146 million
Land area: 17,075,400 square kilometers
(6,592,850 square miles)
Official language: Russian
Main religion: Russian Orthodox Christianity
Currency: Ruble
National holiday: Independence Day (June 12)

(above) Lake Baikal freezes over during the long, frigid Siberian winters.

(opposite) Rugged hills rise above winding rivers in Kamchatka Peninsula.

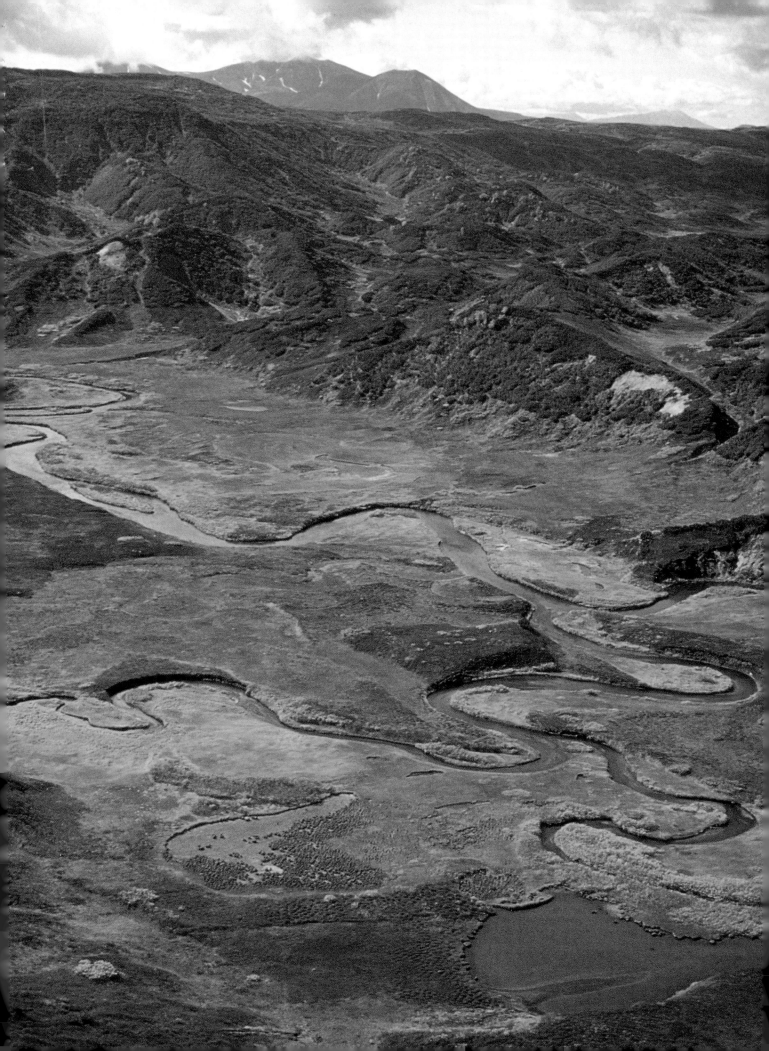

Russia's geographic shape and its government have changed many times throughout the centuries. Its most dramatic changes have happened in the last hundred years. During this time, Russians have made great advancements in **industry**, science, and the arts. They have also suffered through **revolutions**, wars, starvation, and serious **economic** problems.

A lavish staircase leads to the upstairs rooms of the Grand Palace in Petrodvorets, on the outskirts of St. Petersburg. The czars used this palace as a summer home.

Ordinary people, including many women, fought for the Communists during the 1917 revolution.

The time of the czars

For five hundred years, Russia was a powerful **empire** governed by royal emperors called **czars**. The czars lived in luxury, but the lives of the Russian people were miserable. Their anger eventually erupted into a violent revolution that forced the czars from power in 1917. This revolt was led by **Communists**, who took over the country. They believed that the government should own and manage all the country's farms, industries, businesses, and banks. To keep control, they did not allow ordinary people to be politically active. Instead, only members of the Communist Party could influence political life. As well, people were forbidden to express opinions that opposed Communist ideas.

The Soviet Union

Under Communist rule, Russia gradually reconquered fourteen territories in Europe and Asia that were once part of the Russian Empire. These lands belonged to different **ethnic groups**. Each ethnic group shared a common language, religion, and history. Together with Russia, the fourteen territories formed the Union of **Soviet Socialist** Republics (U.S.S.R.), or Soviet Union. Russia ruled this newly industrialized country, which became a military superpower. All citizens had jobs, free education, and health care. Communist rule was harsh though, and many people suffered.

End of the Soviet Union

In the 1980s, the Soviet Union began to experience severe problems. Some people were unhappy with the limits the Communist government placed on their freedoms. They were also frustrated because the government-run farms and factories were outdated and could not make enough food, clothing, and affordable household goods.

When the Communists could not agree with one another about what changes were necessary, the Communist Party fell apart and lost power. Russia and the fourteen other **republics** that made up the Soviet Union split apart to form their own countries. Once the Soviet Union ceased to exist, Russia began to move toward **democracy**. People could finally elect their own representatives to government, and they began to enjoy new freedoms.

(above) Over many decades, the Communist government changed Russia from a farming country into an industrial nation with huge government-owned factories.

(below) People carry a huge Russian flag through Red Square in Moscow to celebrate the end of the Soviet Union and the beginning of an independent Russia, in August 1991.

Largest in the world

Russia is enormous! It stretches half-way around the globe, sits across two continents, and spans eleven time zones. Before people in the far west even get out of bed, those in the far east have finished their day.

Over the centuries, the Volga river has provided Russians with water, food, and transportation. Russians fondly call it **matushka,** *or "mother."*

Quick facts on Russia

- The Kaliningrad Territory along the Baltic Sea is part of Russia, although it is not connected to the main part of the country.

- In the far east, Russia sits just 5.4 kilometers (3.4 miles) from Alaska and 4 kilometers (2.5 miles) from Japan.

- Russia belongs to the Commonwealth of Independent States (C.I.S.). The C.I.S. is made up of twelve countries that belonged to the Soviet Union. Besides Russia, these countries are Ukraine, Belorussia, Moldova, Georgia, Armenia, Azerbaijan, Kazakhstan, Uzbekistan, Kirghizstan, Turkmenistan, and Tadzhikistan.

RUSSIA

The Commonwealth of Independent States

1. Belorussia
2. Ukraine
3. Moldova
4. Georgia
5. Armenia
6. Azerbaijan
7. Kazakhstan
8. Turkmenistan
9. Uzbekistan
10. Tadzhikistan
11. Kirghizstan

The Caucasus Mountains lie south of the European Plain. Their snowy slopes are popular for winter sports.

Land and water

Russia's landscape is filled with sweeping grasslands, broad valleys, mountains, forests, and **tundra**, which is frozen land where no trees grow. Russia is also a country of water. About 200,000 lakes and thousands of rivers link Russia to major seas and oceans. The five main land regions, from west to east, are the European Plain, the Ural Mountains, the West Siberian Plain, the Central Siberian Plateau, and the East Siberian Uplands.

The European Plain

The European Plain is mostly flat or gently rolling land covered by grass and forests. It is home to Russia's largest cities, Moscow and St. Petersburg. The majority of the population, industries, and farmland are found in this region, as is the Volga River, the longest river in Europe.

The Ural Mountains

The Ural Mountain chain divides the continents of Europe and Asia. It also marks the border between the western part of Russia and the eastern part, called Siberia. The Urals are extremely rich in metals and minerals. Many industries based on mining have developed in cities throughout the mountains.

Siberian plains and plateaus

The West Siberian Plain is an enormous, flat region covered with endless forests and grassland. This plain, which is the largest area of flat land in the world, also has some of the world's biggest **bogs**.

The Central Siberian Plateau is a thickly forested region of extremely hot and cold temperatures. Countless streams wind through this area. In the far south, nestled among the peaks of the Sayan and Baikal Mountains, sits Lake Baikal, the largest freshwater lake in the world.

(above) The Ob River floods the West Siberian Plain.

(below) Fields surround a farming village in the rolling Urals.

The Koryak Volcano is one of over 180 volcanoes that crowd the Kamchatka Peninsula.

The East Siberian Uplands

The East Siberian Uplands is an area with mountain ranges such as the Kolyma and Verkhoyansk Mountains. Some ranges jut into the Pacific Ocean, forming **peninsulas**, or narrow pieces of land that project far into the water. The most impressive peninsula is the large Kamchatka, nicknamed "the land of fire and ice." Mostly frozen and covered with snow, Kamchatka also has hot springs and geysers, which gush near-boiling water high into the air.

(above) Gases spew from a vent in a volcano. When the hot gases come in contact with cool air and rock, they harden and form yellowish sulfur deposits.

(below) Lakes start to thaw on the north-eastern edge of Siberia.

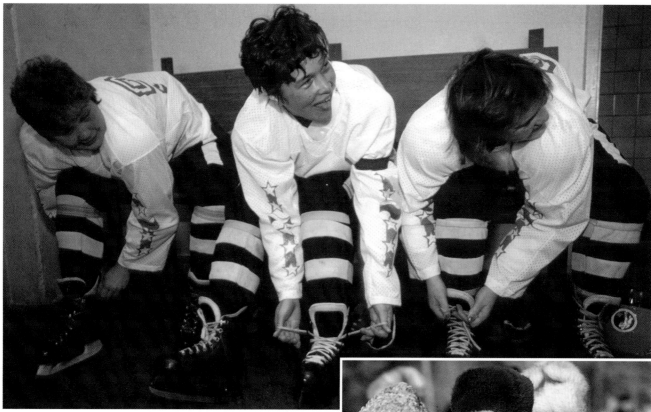

Players from the All-Russia Women's Hockey Team lace up their skates.

Russia is home to over 130 different ethnic groups. Its population is spread unevenly across the country. Three quarters of the people live in the west, while the rest are scattered across Siberia.

Slavic peoples

Most Russians are ethnic Russians, descended from an ancient people called the East Slavs. The East Slavs founded the first Russian land, Kievan Rus, in the ninth century. Ethnic Russians have always played a major role in their country's politics and history. They have also had more **privileges** than other ethnic groups. Most ethnic Russians belong to the Russian Orthodox Church. Russian Orthodoxy is a **denomination** of Christianity, the religion based on the teachings of Jesus Christ, who Christians believe is the son of God.

Russians dressed in warm fur coats and hats meet in a Moscow park.

Two other peoples are descended from the East Slavs — the Ukrainians and Belorussians. Most of these peoples live in the neighboring countries of Ukraine and Belorussia, but millions also live within Russia's borders. Their languages are similar to that of the ethnic Russians, and most follow the Christian religion.

Turkic peoples

After the East Slavs, the next-largest group in Russia is the Turkic peoples. They include Tatars, Chuvash, Bashkir, Sakhas, and Tuvans. These groups speak different Turkic languages. Most Turkic peoples are Muslim. Their religion, Islam, is based on the teachings of the **prophet** Muhammad. Some Turkic peoples follow other religions. For example, the Chuvash are Christians.

Other groups

Among the many other ethnic groups living in Russia are people who are originally from neighboring countries such as Germany, Poland, Lithuania, Latvia, and Estonia. Hundreds of thousands of Jews also live in Russia, but their numbers are dwindling as many **emigrate** to Israel and other countries. The frozen regions in Siberia's far north and east are thinly populated, but a few peoples, including the Inuit, Aleuts, Chukchi, and Evenki, live there.

(right) A Nenets boy, from northwest Siberia, waits to go fishing with his father. The Nenets people have traditionally been fishers and reindeer herders.

(below) Russian grandmothers, or **babushkas**, *read and chat outdoors in northeast Siberia.*

Plants and animals

Three main zones of vegetation, or plant life, stretch across Russia. Each zone has its own type of wildlife. From south to north, these zones are the **steppes**, forests, and tundra.

When this mother bear's cub is an adult, it will weigh more than 1000 times its birth weight.

Steppes and forests

Most of Russia's southern regions are steppes, or grasslands, where animals such as antelope, foxes, and gray partridges live. North of the steppes, and far up the sides of many mountains, lie Russia's immense forests. The majority of Russia's forests are **taiga** — dense, swampy woodlands with spruce, pine, and other conifers, or cone-bearing trees. Russia's forests are home to many mammals, including huge populations of deer, elk, beavers, wolves, and the country's best-known animal, the brown bear.

The Russian bear

Brown bears have sharp hearing, excellent eyesight, and a strong sense of smell. They have huge appetites, and eat whatever they find, whether meat or vegetable. During Russia's long, barren winters, brown bears nestle in their dens and fall into a hibernation-like sleep that conserves their energy until spring. Unlike animals that truly hibernate, brown bears can wake up in just minutes if they are in danger!

The musk ox's long, thick fur protects it from Siberia's blizzards and howling winds.

The Siberian tiger

Another famous forest animal, the Siberian tiger, lives in the mountains in Russia's far east. Siberian tigers can survive in even the coldest temperatures and are superb winter hunters. Their hind legs are longer than their front legs, allowing them to easily bound through deep snow. Unfortunately, humans have hunted these animals almost to **extinction**. Only about 300 survive in the wild.

Treeless tundra

Far in the north, along the coast of the Arctic Ocean, lies the tundra. Covering nearly a quarter of Russia, the tundra is so cold that, even in summertime, only the surface of the marshy soil thaws. Beneath the surface is **permafrost**, or ground that remains frozen year-round. Many animals have adapted to life in the harsh tundra, including Arctic foxes, hares, and mouse-like lemmings. One of the largest tundra inhabitants is the reindeer, the only deer species in which both males and females have antlers.

The snowy owl's speckled plumage helps it blend in with the rocks and snow of its habitat.

The Siberian tiger is the world's largest cat, weighing up to 300 kilograms (660 pounds).

Lake Baikal

Lake Baikal, in south-central Russia, is nicknamed the "Blue Eye of Siberia." It is one of the most remarkable places on earth. Reaching depths of up to 1.6 kilometers (1 mile), it holds more water than any other lake in the world. Lake Baikal is not just exceptional for its size. It is well-known for its fascinating plants and animals, and for its stunning beauty.

Nowhere else on earth

Plants and animals thrive in and around the pure, clear water of Lake Baikal. About 1100 types of plants and 1550 types of animal live here, many of which are not found anywhere else on the planet. To learn about and preserve the lake's unique wildlife, Russian scientists created their own field of study, called "baikalology," named after Lake Baikal.

The Baikal seal

The lake's only mammal, the nerpa or Baikal seal, is one of the world's smallest seals. It is also one of the few seals that lives in fresh water instead of salt water. How Baikal seals reached the lake is a mystery. Most scientists believe that Lake Baikal is too far from the ocean for the seals to have swum there or to have crossed over land. In recent years, many Baikal seals have died from an unknown cause, worrying scientists and visitors to the lake.

The golomyanka

More than 50 species of fish live in the lake, including sturgeon, salmon, and whitefish. Many of these fish are caught by the local people for food. One of the lake's most interesting fish is the golomyanka. The golomyanka lives between 1 to 1.5 kilometers (0.6 to 0.9 miles) below the surface during the day. At night, it swims to the top of the water to dine on tiny creatures called plankton. The golomyanka's transparent body is made largely of fat. If it is still at the surface when the sun comes out, the sun's warmth will cause the fat to melt and the golomyanka's body will turn into an oily blob.

Baikal seals like to bask in the sun when they are not swimming.

(opposite) Lake Baikal's shoreline stretches over 2100 km (1300 miles). Over 300 rivers and streams feed the lake, but only one river, the Angara, flows out.

Holy Baikal

People have been drawn to Lake Baikal for centuries because of its beauty. In the past, **pilgrims**, or travelers on journeys to **holy** sites, visited the lake because they believed that it was filled with powerful spirits and energy. Today, Lake Baikal continues to attract pilgrims, as well as tourists who come to relax at a local resort.

Protecting a treasure

To protect Lake Baikal and its wildlife, the Russian government has passed tough laws restricting development and pollution around the lake. Scientists fear that any pollution, no matter how small the amount, may threaten the purity of the lake's waters and harm its delicate wildlife.

(right) For the past 30 years, scientists and local residents have been protesting the expansion of a pulp plant close to Lake Baikal's shore.

(below) Freshwater sponges grow at the bottom of Lake Baikal.

Russia is one of the coldest places in the world. Its long, snowy winters are a time of frigid winds, called *purgas*, and blizzards, or *burans*. For at least six months each year, people must dress in heavy boots, bulky coats, furry hats, and thick gloves. Many Russians love winter, despite the snow and ice. Even in cold weather, they enjoy a brisk walk, stopping outdoors for coffee or ice cream!

Russia's freezing winter temperatures are caused in part by its northerly location. As well, mountains in the west, east, and south block almost all the warm air that blows from the Atlantic, Indian, and Pacific Oceans. Instead, very cold, dry air blows from the Arctic Ocean.

(right) A fur hat with ear flaps, called a **shapka**, *keeps this girl warm in even the coldest weather.*

(below) During the long winters, much of interior Siberia seems endlessly flat and white.

Winter's grip

In the heart of winter, many parts of the country look very peaceful and beautiful, covered with icicles and a sparkling blanket of snow. Rivers and lakes freeze over with a thick layer of ice. Some places, especially in northeast Siberia, have temperatures as low as –71°C (–96°F). Skin exposed to these temperatures can freeze within minutes, so people in these areas spend most of their time indoors.

Suddenly summer

Russia is sometimes described as having only two seasons, winter and summer, because spring and autumn are so short. No other country experiences such an extreme range of temperatures. Compared to the deadly lows of winter, summer temperatures can rise as high as 38°C (100°F).

(above) Children often spend snowy weekends playing outside.

On a warm summer day, sunbathers crowd a beach on the Neva River in St. Petersburg.

Russia's cities are very different from one another. Older cities are filled with beautiful buildings constructed centuries ago. Other cities, especially in Siberia, are younger, steel-and-cement industrial centers. Russia's two largest cities, Moscow and St. Petersburg, have changed since Soviet times. Streets formerly lined with plain, government-run businesses are now alive with street vendors, Western-style stores and restaurants, and colorful billboards. Unfortunately, there are also more homeless people and more crime.

Magnificent Moscow

Moscow is Russia's largest city. It is the country's **capital**, and the center of business, culture, and the Russian Orthodox Church. Thousands of people move to Moscow each year to look for work, making it very crowded. Most of the city's nine million citizens, called Muscovites, live in row upon row of concrete apartment buildings built by the government after World War II ended in 1945.

(above) Most of Moscow's apartments are cramped, so many tenants convert their balconies into extra rooms.

(below) Bundled in her winter coat, a mother reads as her child naps in one of Moscow's many parks.

Heart of the capital

Moscow's history goes back over 850 years to the time when settlers built a *kreml*, or fortress, on the banks of the Moskva River. Today, this structure, called the Kremlin, is the heart of the city. Inside the Kremlin are old and beautiful churches, gardens, and some of Russia's government buildings. Outside is Red Square, a favorite place for large gatherings and national parades.

(above) Buildings and churches crowd the streets of downtown Moscow.

(right) In 1990, McDonald's opened its first restaurant in the Soviet Union. Fast food is popular in Moscow, although it is very expensive.

(below) Guards march through Red Square past Lenin's tomb. The preserved body of the first leader of the Communist Party has been on display since 1930, but may soon be buried.

Water is everywhere in St. Petersburg. The city was built on a hundred islands in the Neva River delta.

Stunning St. Petersburg

St. Petersburg was founded in 1703 by Czar Peter the Great. He built the city as a symbol of the Russian empire's power and beauty. St. Petersburg, which was also known as Petrograd and Leningrad in the 1900s, served as the country's capital from 1712 to 1918. The city is filled with stunning palaces, sculptures, and fountains. St. Petersburg is also a well-known center for ballet, music, and literature.

White nights

St. Petersburg is located in the far north where, for three weeks each June, it is light for almost 24 hours of the day. The sun sets at 2:00 a.m. and rises at 2:30 a.m, with only a half hour of twilight in between. These "White Nights" are celebrated with festivals of music and dancing.

Catherine the Great's palace in Pushkin, a suburb of St. Petersburg, reflects the Czaritza's lavish taste.

(above) In the city of Nizhny Novgorod, a Russian Orthodox cathedral sits next to loading docks on the Volga River.

(left) Irkutsk, a city in south-central Russia, is home to nearly half a million people.

(below) Vladivostok is a major naval base on the Pacific Coast.

A changing economy

Since the early 1990s, Russia's post-Communist government has been making major changes to the economy. Instead of owning all of Russia's industries and controlling the prices of all goods, the government is slowly handing over its farms, factories, businesses, and banks to private businesses which compete with one another for customers.

Difficult times

While a few Russians have grown wealthy under the new **free-market** economy, the country as a whole has not prospered. Most people are earning less than before. Millions have lost their jobs because many new businesses and old government factories could not earn a profit and were forced to shut down. Without government controls on prices, the cost of food has increased so much that some people can afford to eat only bread and tea. Even with these hardships, many Russians believe that life will eventually improve.

A transport truck is loaded with lumber at a port on Sakhalin Island, off Russia's southeastern coast.

Shoppers can buy the latest fashions at the large GUM department store in Moscow.

New business

Thousands of Russians have started new businesses in recent years, something that was illegal during the Soviet era. Wealthy Russians have invested in large businesses such as factories, mines, and oil companies. Most new businesses, however, are small. They include restaurants, hair salons, and sidewalk stalls, where people of all ages sell magazines, home-made crafts, and fruit and vegetables that they grow in their gardens in the countryside.

A fur coat stall in an outdoor market is very popular with people preparing for winter!

Abundant resources

Russia's natural resources lie mostly untapped in hard-to-reach parts of Siberia. They include vast forests and huge deposits of minerals such as gold, diamonds, iron ore, copper, nickel, and lead. The country also has large **reserves** of coal, natural gas, and oil. Much of the equipment used to **extract** these resources is old-fashioned, wasteful, and sometimes dangerous. To modernize these industries, Russia is seeking partnerships with foreign companies that specialize in forestry, mining, and energy.

Heavy industry and manufacturing

The most important parts of Russia's economy are heavy industry and manufacturing, both based mainly around Moscow and St. Petersburg. Heavy industries make raw materials into steel, chemicals, **petroleum**, and plastics. Manufacturing plants and factories use these products to build machinery, motor vehicles, and other equipment. In Soviet times, Russia's factories built mainly military equipment and weapons. Today, factories are being updated to produce more consumer goods such as radios, hair dryers, and furniture, as well as construction materials and medical supplies.

Many people work in the manufacturing industry, making useful, everyday products such as boots.

Farming and fishing

Russia has enormous areas of rich farmland. Its long coasts and rivers link it to some of the world's largest stocks of seafood. Like all other parts of the economy, Russia's farming and fishing industries are changing to the free-market system. The government still owns most Russian farms, but it is trying to encourage farmers to buy them as private businesses. Today, about half of Russia's farms are managed by the people who work there. The rest are run by the government.

Fertile farmland

Russia is one of the world's top producers of grains such as wheat and barley. These crops, which thrive in Russia's short, dry summer, grow mainly in the steppes. In the lush Caucasus Mountains, farmers plant cherries, apricots, melons, and other fruits and vegetables. In Siberia, where the growing season is too short for crops, families often grow fruit and vegetables in greenhouses. Throughout the country, farmers raise cattle, pigs, chickens, and other livestock for meat, eggs, and milk.

So much food!

One of the greatest challenges farmers hope to solve is waste. Russia's farms produce huge amounts of food, but much spoils before it gets to market because there is no efficient system to store, transport, and package it.

(left) A tractor adds to a huge pile of harvested beets.

(top) Herders milk goats in the Caucasus Mountains.

Fishing fleets

Large Russian fishing fleets sail the country's rivers, lakes, and oceans. They haul in vast catches of seafood, including salmon, haddock, cod, and herring. Many of the country's largest ships are like floating factories. Fishers can clean and **process** their catches on board. Russia's most famous seafood is caviar. This salty delicacy is made from the eggs of the sturgeon fish, caught mainly in the Volga River and Caspian Sea.

The number of fish in Russia and throughout the world has shrunk in recent years due to pollution and overfishing. Because of smaller fish stocks and increasing competition from other countries' fishing fleets, Russia's fishers have been hauling in smaller and smaller catches.

*(above) Many Russian families with small weekend cottages, called **dachas**, have vegetable gardens where they grow some of their own food.*

(below) Fishermen haul in a large catch of salmon. They have had a very successful day!

Transportation

If you are not in the city, getting from one place to another in Russia is a challenge! Cities have good public transit services, such as buses, streetcars, and subway trains. In the countryside, however, people have to travel great distances in difficult weather to reach their destinations.

Russia has few highways, and paved roads are rare outside of cities. Only one of every twenty Russians owns an automobile. Instead, people walk, cycle, or use snowmobiles, trains, and boats to get around. In some rural places, horse-drawn wagons and, very rarely, traditional three-horse sleighs called *troikas* are used for travel. Flying on a plane or helicopter is often the only way to get to the most remote parts of the country.

(above) Streetcars are one of the easiest ways to get around St. Petersburg.

(top) Some peoples of the Arctic, such as the Nentsy, still travel by reindeer sled.

A Trans-Siberian Railway train makes its way across the expanse of south-central Siberia.

On the water

A network of **canals** connect Russia's cities to rivers and seas. These water routes are important shipping paths, although some northern rivers are frozen over for several months each year. Major seaports, such as St. Petersburg, Vladivostock, and Murmansk, are kept open as long as possible during the winter by huge, powerful ships that break up the pack ice.

A cyclist in snowy St. Petersburg waits for a freight train to pass at a railway crossing.

The Trans-Siberian Railway

Many rail systems carry goods and passengers across the western part of Russia. Only one major line crosses the huge expanse of Siberia. The Trans-Siberian Railway runs between Moscow and Vladivostock, on the Pacific coast. At 9240 kilometers (5747 miles), it covers about a third of the distance around the planet. It took over fifteen years to construct the line, which was completed in 1905. Many workers died laying the tracks due to terrible accidents, the extreme Siberian climate, and the lack of proper food and water.

All aboard!

Passengers riding the Trans-Siberian spend between seven and ten days on comfortable trains with sleeping compartments and a dining car. Along the way, they pass through seven time zones and make over 90 stops at cities, towns, and remote villages. During a stop, many passengers get off the train to buy tasty homemade meals sold by local women along the train platform. Stops are just a few minutes long, and the train gives just one warning blast before departing. Passengers must get back on board quickly so they are not left behind!

Russia became a world leader in space exploration in 1957 when, as part of the Soviet Space Agency, it launched Sputnik 1, the world's first artificial **satellite**. Today, the Russian Space Agency's main goals include improving telephone, television, and weather forecasting services with new satellites, and playing a major role in the construction of the International Space Station (ISS). The Russian Space Agency has had to scale back some of its plans, however, due to a shortage of funding.

The space race

The launch of Sputnik 1 stunned the world and was a triumph for Soviet **cosmonauts**, or astronauts. Shortly after, they launched Sputnik 2, which carried the first passenger — a dog named Laika — into space. Although Laika lived only a week, Sputnik 2 was considered another great success. To compete with the Soviets in space exploration, the United States created NASA, the National Aeronautics and Space Administration. Over the next 30 years, the two countries raced to be the first to make important space breakthroughs. This competition was called the Space Race.

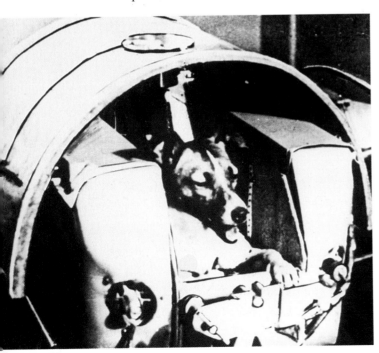

The Mir space station

For decades, the Soviet Union worked to put a permanent space station in orbit. In 1986, it launched Mir, which means "peace." Mir became the longest-running and most successful space station ever. During its thirteen-year mission, crew members from Russia and other countries visited the space station. Mir hosted countless science experiments, docked with American space shuttles, and even survived a fire and a crash with a small cargo ship.

Space firsts

The Soviets scored many important firsts in space, including:

 the first moon probe (Luna 1, 1959)

 the first human in space and the first human to orbit the earth (Yuri Gagarin, aboard Vostock 1, 1961)

the first woman in space (Valentina Tereshkova, aboard Vostock 6, 1963)

the first docking of two crewed spacecrafts and exchange of crews (Soyuz 4 and Soyuz 5, 1969)

the first experimental space station (Salyut 1, 1971)

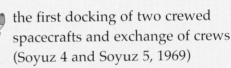 the longest consecutive stay in space (438 days by Valery Polyakov, aboard Mir, 1994)

Laika sits in her air-conditioned cabin ready to blast off on Sputnik 2.

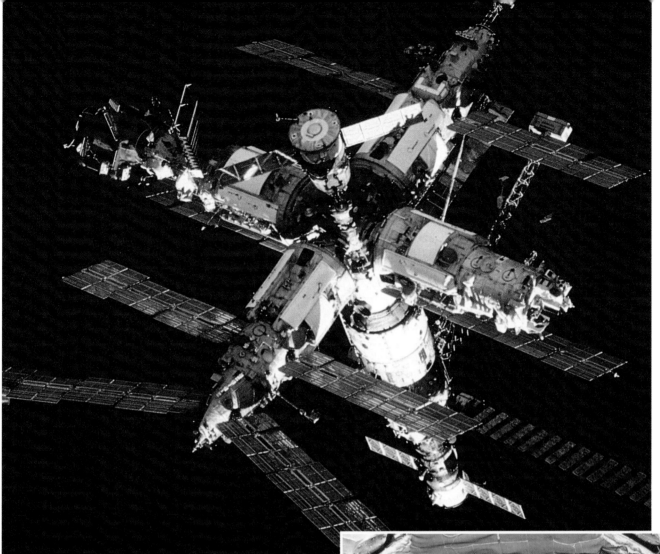

The Mir space station prepares for a docking with a space shuttle bringing supplies.

Life aboard Mir

Scientists on Mir learned valuable lessons about what it is like to live for long periods of time in space. Crew members had a work area, a small kitchen, bedrooms, and a bathroom, complete with toilet and shower. When not performing experiments or fixing the space station, the crew relaxed. They exercised, looked at Earth through a porthole, sent messages to their families, or had fun floating around in the weightless atmosphere.

The International Space Station

Russia is an important member of the team of countries working on the new International Space Station. These countries hope that the ISS will continue Mir's mission of studying life on Earth and in space.

Russian cosmonauts Anatoly Solovyev and Nikolai Budarin take a last look at the departing crew of the Atlantis space shuttle before closing Mir's hatch.

 # Glossary

bog An area of soft, wet land

canal A man-made river

capital A city where the government of a state or country is located

Communist A person who believes in an economic system where the country's natural resources, businesses, and industries are owned and controlled by the government

cosmonaut A Soviet or Russian astronaut

czar The title given to Russian emperors

democracy A form of government in which representatives are elected to make decisions for a society

denomination An organized religious group within a faith

economic Dealing with the way a country organizes and manages its businesses, industries, and money

emigrate To move to a new country

empire A group of countries or territories having the same ruler

ethnic group A group of people who share a common race, language, heritage, or religion

extinction When a type of animal or species no longer exists

extract To remove something from its natural place, like oil from the earth

free-market Trade without high taxes or strict government control

holy Having special religious importance

industry The making of things using factories

natural resources Materials found in nature, such as oil, coal, minerals, and lumber, which are useful to humans

peninsula A point of land that juts into a body of water

permafrost Land in cold climates that remains frozen all year long

petroleum A dark liquid found underground that is used to create gasoline and other fuels

pilgrim A person who makes a religious journey to a holy place

privilege A special right

process To treat or prepare something by a special method

prophet A person who is believed to speak on behalf of God

republic A country that is not led by a king or queen

reserve A large supply of an item stored for future use

revolution An uprising or war against a government

satellite A man-made object that revolves around the earth or other bodies in space

Socialist Following an economic system where the country's natural resources, businesses, industries, and politics are controlled by the entire community

Soviet Having to do with, or a citizen of, the Union of Soviet Socialist Republics (U.S.S.R.), which existed from 1922 to 1991

steppes A large, treeless plain

taiga Damp, swampy forests

tundra A large plain where little vegetation grows and which remains frozen all year

Index

1 2 3 4 5 6 7 8 9 0   Printed in the USA   5 4 3 2 1 0